SERIES "Fearless Tales for Growing Minds"
Copyright Message:
© 2025 ALINA STETSYUK

All rights reserved. No part of this publication may be reproduced, distributed, or transmitted in any form or by any means, including photocopying, recording, or other electronic or mechanical methods, without the prior written permission of the publisher, except in the case of brief quotations embodied in critical reviews and certain other noncommercial uses permitted by copyright law.

For permissions requests or inquiries, contact
alinastetsyukwriter@gmail.com

Dear Readers,

Welcome to Fearless Tales for Growing Minds — a collection of stories crafted to spark courage, inspire curiosity, and nurture wisdom in every young heart and mind.

Within these pages, you'll meet characters who face their fears with quiet bravery, navigate challenges with clever thinking, and discover the transformative power of kindness, gratitude, and resilience. Each tale is more than just a story — it's a gentle guide, offering lessons that linger long after the final page is turned.

The word fearless here isn't about being unafraid — it's about stepping forward despite fear, speaking up when it's hard, and believing in your voice. And growing minds aren't just about getting smarter — they're about understanding emotions, building connections, and embracing every experience as a chance to succeed.

Every story in this collection holds a mirror to life's little and big moments, showing that courage comes in many forms and that even the smallest choices can shape our journey in profound ways.

So, dear reader, settle in, turn the page, and let these tales remind you of the strength, kindness, and endless possibility within you.

Warm regards,
Alina Stetsyuk

Deep in a magical forest, where tall pine trees whispered in the wind, and streams giggled over smooth stones, lived Luna, the spirit of the woods.

Luna wasn't just a girl. She was part of the forest. As light as a breeze and as quiet as starlight. Her big glowing eyes sparkled in the dark like two little lanterns. But Luna didn't think her eyes were special. She thought they were weird.

While the raccoons scurried for food, the coyotes zoomed through the brush, and the squirrels flipped through the trees, Luna just sat quietly, hiding.

— "All I have are these strange, glowing eyes…" she sighed, staring at her reflection in the still lake.

But one night, something scary happened. Dark clouds covered the sky, hiding every star. Even the moon disappeared. The forest turned pitch-black.

A group of young animals who had been playing near the trees got lost and couldn't find their way home. They cried out, calling for help.

Luna heard them. Her heart raced. — "What if they laugh at me again?" she whispered, frozen with fear.

But then she remembered the little baby deer who had just learned to walk. The deer couldn't find its way in the dark without help.
Luna took a deep breath.
— "This is no time to hide," she said to herself.

She stepped forward and opened her eyes. Instantly, they lit up with golden light! A warm glow filled the forest, lighting up the path like a dream. The lost animals looked up, surprised, and ran toward the sound of their families.

The raccoons, coyotes, and squirrels stared in wonder.
— "You saved us!" cried a small raccoon.

From that night on, everything changed for Luna. She didn't hide anymore. She realized her glowing eyes weren't weird — they were powerful!

Luna helped the forest in every way she could. She lit paths for travellers, showed the young owls not to fear the dark, and taught everyone how their own special talents could help others.

Bonus Story
Luna and the Storm

One day, a mighty storm rolled over the forest. Luna didn't face it alone.

The squirrels used their nimble paws to fix nests.
The beavers built strong dams to stop the river from flooding.

The bats listened carefully and warned everyone of danger with their sharp hearing.

Together, they weathered the storm.
When the sun returned, and the forest calmed, the animals understood something important:

Their greatest strength was their ability to work together and trust one another. Even if you're different, your gift might be exactly what the world needs.

From then on, Luna wasn't just the spirit of the forest — she became a legend. A light that helped guide the lost animals home.

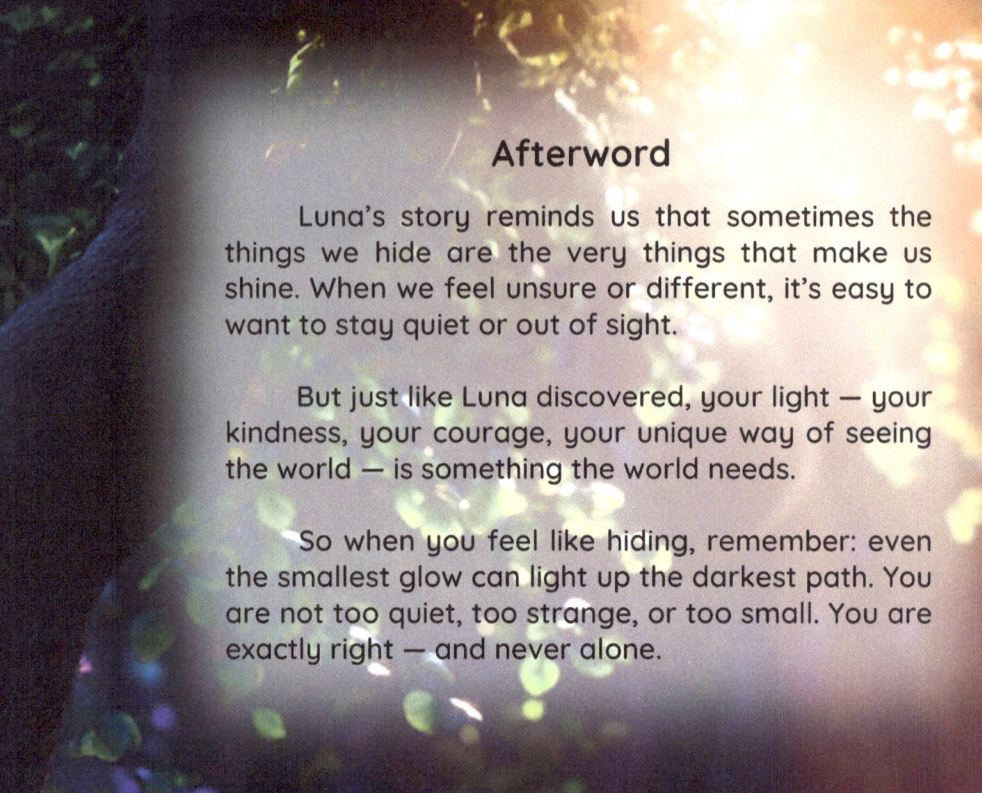

Afterword

Luna's story reminds us that sometimes the things we hide are the very things that make us shine. When we feel unsure or different, it's easy to want to stay quiet or out of sight.

But just like Luna discovered, your light — your kindness, your courage, your unique way of seeing the world — is something the world needs.

So when you feel like hiding, remember: even the smallest glow can light up the darkest path. You are not too quiet, too strange, or too small. You are exactly right — and never alone.

Parent & Child Activity: Shine with Luna!
Strengthen Your Bond—Glow, Share, and Celebrate
What Makes You Special!

1. **Shine Spotlight Game:** Take turns saying, "One thing that makes me special is…"
Then say something special about the other person!
Ask: "When do you feel like your light shines the brightest?"

2. **Luna's Lantern Drawing:** Draw a lantern or glowing orb on paper. Inside, write or draw the things that make you you — talents, kind actions, or even quiet strengths.
Hang it somewhere to remind you to keep glowing!

3. **Hide & Shine!:** Play a gentle hide-and-seek game. When someone is "found," they share something they're proud of or something they've recently done that was brave or kind.

4. **Night Glow Walk:** Take a short walk in the evening (even just around your home). Talk about what makes nighttime special — and what would make someone feel safe or brave in the dark.

5. **Encourage-a-Friend Letter:** Help your child write a short letter or draw a picture for someone they know who might be shy or unsure.
Ask: "What could we say to help someone feel brave and seen?"